To see HIM

A Poetic and Contemplative View of Life,
Being Present to HIS Presence

$\longleftrightarrow$

Robert A. Dorsch O.F.S.

WestBow Press books may be ordered through booksellers or by contacting:

WestBow Press
A Division of Thomas Nelson & Zondervan
1663 Liberty Drive
Bloomington, IN 47403
www.westbowpress.com
1 (866) 928-1240

Interior Image Credit: Robert A. Dorsch OFS and Andrea Mae Doub, Dr. Veronica Vezzani

ISBN: 978-1-9736-7219-7 (sc)
ISBN: 978-1-9736-7220-3 (e)

Library of Congress Control Number: 2019911778

Print information available on the last page.

WestBow Press rev. date: 08/27/2019

WestBow
PRESS
A DIVISION OF THOMAS NELSON
& ZONDERVAN

I am ever grateful to all those who caused me to be who I am today. God, my loving parents, my incredible wife, my amazing children with their families, my faithful fraternity, and my siblings. Thank you all.

I recently read a passage that summarizes my perspective well:

"God is present in everything. In the universe, in creation, in me and all that happens to me, in my brothers and sisters, in the church, and in the Eucharist". —Thea Bowman

Thea Bowman: A Gift to the Church," Modern Spiritual Masters: Writings on Contemplation and Compassion, ed. Robert Ellsberg (Orbis Books: 2008),

My Outside Place

Sitting in my outside place
The red bird pierces the morning silence
First very near then not so
Many feathered friends join with song

The sun persuades the the morning sky
The cool morning air challenges my outside place
Yet the red bird continues its insistent plea
Its brilliant red flits through the various greens

Flowers so brilliant with varied plants
All grace HIS outside
The dew drips from the decorative grass
Again the red bird's plea
All in my outside place.

Mountain Stream

Standing in this Mtn steam
The mist yields to the morning rays
The waning scent of wild roses
A new bloom of laurel makes itself known

Bowing through the narrow rhododendron
The stream deepens the water calms
Distant rapids share their calming melody
Here in HIS mountain stream

The Jay harshly announces its displeasure
A brown trout lurks determined
Blossoms of all types cascade toward the water
The shadow of an osprey glides across this mountain stream

The sun gets higher in the sky, clouds begin to grow
A breeze, no a wind comes through the trees
A mosaic of leaves cover the water and begin their slow journey
The crows deliver an endless shrill cacophony
A king fisher chatters as it glides, swoops, dives climbing its way along the bank
All while standing in this mountain stream

Concrete and Asphalt

Concrete and asphalt surround
A service rep tests a mustang gt
The hat backwards the motor growls
Heads turn old men smile and nod

People come people go
HIS sparrows tweet with glee
At home on the steel edifice
Men chat exchanging life stories
Surrounded by concrete and asphalt

A mother sits with an infant in her arms
Chatting on the phone, her 3 yr old transparent
Yearning for attention but only gets a "stop Beau"
A constant barrage of stop, don't, come here
Nay a drop of love or positive word

Harried they rush in, ear to the phone
Only to rush out and on to the next
Hand in hand a couple walk unaware of the buzz about
Such a contrast of priorities and perspectives
All surrounded by concrete and asphalt

Sea Breeze

The steady sea breeze
Accompanied by the rhythms of the water
Punctuated by squeals and joyful sounds
To be like HIS children is the charge

Gruff laughter rings out
Dogs chat with each other
A ball bounces without purpose across the sand
All in this steady sea breeze.

A mother rat scurries with young
Children test their courage in the shallow
How many years has this ritual repeated
Yet the cadence of the water unchanged

Footprints vanish almost as quick as created
Caring adults are ever vigilant, teaching and loving
Snacks, juice box and sun screen
The steady sea breeze surrounds

The Day Begins

As the day begins
The never ending waves deliver their melodious song
Stubborn clouds attempt to restrain the sun
Few meander along the surf
Picking at shells like chickens in the field

What makes a shell deserving
Can one be better than the other
All created with awesome life
Contributing to the world in their small but critical way

A fisherman search's for the perfect spot
The sun finally triumphs with all its splendor
People all with their individual thoughts walk
Walk with trials, triumphs, joys, heavy hearts,but all walk

The sounds, smells, touch, all seem like a potent medicine
Perhaps people do feel small
Perhaps HIS presence is felt by some
Perhaps for the first time as the day begins

Mother Nature

When Mother Nature shows
Ebony tones dominated the North sky
Clouds boiled, rolled and twisted
The south sky was oblivious

Winds battled and clouds danced
The sand moved across the beach in sheets
Waves crested, mist moved in concert with the sand
Distant booms announced the severity

Beach goers scattered with haste
Drops of rain foretold the impending
First few and small then large and pounding
Blinding Jagged bolts of light ripped the horizon

Claps of deafening thunder came and went
Rolling along and rumbling with a life their own
HIS life giving water soaked the dry earth
All this Mother Nature showed

Summer Festival

In these Mid West summer festivals
Crowds clog the streets looking for that long sought
Children draw, paint and learn
A woman focused on an ice cream cone is absorbed

The smells of popcorn encompass a corner
Standing with a cowboy hat and a huge mustache
A man smiles Announces cowboy popcorn samples
Another cowboy stirs a kettle wincing at the heat

Artisans with their best work
Eager, sharing, explaining, showing and selling
The strawberry theme is there
Shortcake, brats, beer all strawberry
Smiles, smiles, so many escape, enjoy HIS, why not

A band filters through the malaise
Dancing, singing, laughing and hugging
An older woman sits quietly with her hat
Tapping her foot, smiling and recalling yesteryear
All in this Mid West summer festival.

The Country

Driving through the mid West Country
Red barns with white trim dot the landscape
Their silos stand as sentinels
Seeming to watch, some with Ivey

Tall tan sand hill cranes are easily seen
Foraging in the young corn fields
A flock of snow geese circle a fresh cut field
Effortlessly floating and gliding searching a landing

Red wing blackbirds evict a red tail from their nesting site
Undaunted by size their courage prevails
This Native American paradise holds true HIS
Oneida, Fond du lac, Oconomowac and Waukesha all recall

Drooping Willows stand as companions along the many ponds
Majestic spruce stand guard around the farm houses
The cottonwood shed their fluffy bloom with every breeze
Red maples do their best and brighten all through this mid West Country

Small Town

Small town life and love
With children riding bicycles to and fro
Supper clubs,unique, stand as local monuments
Gathering places for life experience sharing

Towering oak reveal the longevity and history
Names and faces change but the town endures
A cemetery with small markers in a forgotten corner
All paint a storied collage of community

Aged barns sag under the pressure of Time and snow
Wind turbines slowly turn effortlessly together
Dotting the view as far as one can see
Capturing HIS whisper along the lake, a symbol of new

American flags line the streets
Home made signs proclaim yard sales
The fire department reminds all of the annual picnic
Every piece created by small town life and love.

HIS Hand

You'll understand when you hold HIS hand
A priest announced from the pulpit
The Texas heat made the cool air welcoming
A small child fidgeted with mamas watch

The choir so large and talented
3 guitars, 2 horns and a flute listened and waited
The director stood quiet and listened
You'll understand when you hold HIS hand

The pastor and young friar listened
A young girl counts her goldfish
Her infant sister asleep and smiling
A mother rubs her adult, special needs, sons forehead, he smiles

2 young first communicants, hands folded, listen
Their parents so proud listen
All challenged by many examples and hear
You'll understand when you hold HIS hand

Time

Time is interesting and prized
Young cant wait for a birthday
Slowly it moves, but alas it moves as it will
Soon a decade has clicked past

Others work hard day after day
Doing whats right because its right
Children, games, vacations, weddings, picnics and funerals
Joy and sadness all guided by HIS hand

Such moments stack up with time
Memories cherished, lessons taught, lessons learned
A limited commodity, yet treasured?
Wise folk cant believe the speed

Celebrated history vanishes in a blink
Look into the bright eyes of that wise person
As you feed them and ask
Isn't time interesting and prized?

Divine Self

All with HIS divine Self
To see HIM in all life
Drown out by society noise
Blinded by the daily drone

Such a gift to see
What splendor is revealed
Pausing to experience
All with HIS divine self

So many miss the chance
Tangled in lists, screens and self
Hurry to the next, to the next
What about here, what about now?

Do you see HIM
If you look in their eyes?
Appreciate with gratitude the great oak
All with HIS divine self.

At The Store

People scramble for parking spots at this store
A pick up parks in the shade
The horse trailer open
The horse looking out as the driver texts

Hurriedly folks assemble at this store
A young couple excitedly plans dinner
A child revels in her mother's snack choice
The bread vendor smiles and fills the shelves

A family tops off a cart
The children clammer for animal soap at this store
Dad struggles, his scalp with surgery scars
A older lady,trembling, reads a label holding it close

The pharmacist peers over his glasses
Walking like Mick Jagger, a man shouts to his gal
Alas HE is in all of them at this store
HIS presence seen, people at this store

My Gift

Always a smile and a bounce
My gift is always there
Willing, kind, persistent and loving
I take a breath, stop and appreciate

My gift is always there, rain or shine
She is selfless in all she does
Grand-baby, children, friends all
Receive love from my gift

Rare are those like her
Quick to hug and say "I Love You"
What did I do to deserve such
Fortune has smiled upon me

HIS presence can be seen, felt and heard
Kind to all, working hard unceasingly
Always thinking of the other always
What a treasure I have in my gift

Gentle Rain

The gentle rain softly dimples the pond
Yellow poplar leaves yield and float down
The sun gains the upper hand
Rays brighten the dam

A rooster crows defiantly in the distance
Trees wet with HIS life giving water
Seem to rejoice and give thanks
Now a breeze dances in the leaves

Ferns tucked in the corner
Reach up with seemingly new desire
The ground around them
Polka dotted with fallen yellow leaves
This gentle rain marking the time
As the fall draws nearer
The plant life signals their transition ever so deftly

Now the sun has triumphed
The dimples on the water cease
Several fish begin to Top feed
All on this pond in this gentle rain.

Mr. Rob

Sitting in his red office swivel chair, high arms
Desk covered with papers, all with lines and numbers
The market analysis is ongoing
An antique lamp, an office phone and an old flashlight

Make a put, place a call
Numbers flash across 2 screens, slowly scrutinized
Eye glasses slightly low, he talks in a soft voice
Not directly, but expresses thanks for HIS blessings

A vintage stapler and pencil sharpener sit on a shelf
Peanut butter, ritz crackers and empty jelly jar speak
Company welcome, get caught up stories abound
Well worn shoes sit neatly next

Slightly hunched from the years
He smiles and says next Friday I'll be 83
Sticky pie is my favorite, but sour cream coconut cake too
All sitting in his red office chair

Dads Window

His daily sequence lands Dad a seat at his window
Coffee and iPad at the ready, the parade begins
Meal worm, suet, fresh orange, nectar jar and a seed tube
All create a feathered collage second to none

A bright orange oriole, a gold finch so sharp their plumage
Sparrows build a nest in the pine, cardinals court
Mama grosbeak brown,striped breast, gold underwing yellow beak on suet
Humming birds mimic medieval knights,jousting

The second clutch of bluebirds has come of age
Without warning one fledged, lights in the apple tree
Daddy bird's watchful eye ever ready to spurn a hungry intruder
Sitting high atop the near pine

Behind the known and trusted nest yet the wings flick
Encouraging calls from the parents coax the others
One by one they emerge, a strange new world
HIS hand so vividly displayed here out Dads window.

"Witnessed the second batch of b/b. Fledge today. What a beautiful thing
to set 8 new birds off to continue the bluebird future. I thanked God for my
vision to witness this in my 84th year." RGD

The Long, Dark Night

How long is a dark night in HIS hand
Some seem to wake in a wink
The entire night has passed by
Others quite a different perspective

What about the lady that rolled her truck 6 times
Is there night and day, time does pass
Win one small battle just to have another begin
In the end her spouse is keenly attentive

How long is a dark night ask the ALS patient
Finally asleep only to be rousted by stabbing nerve pain
Unrelenting, first one, then two doses, another med, quick, the pain
Morphine finally wins this wretched and insidious battle

So you have minor surgery recovery
Is your night truly a dark night
Just a week or two and normality sneaks back in
All have HIM close on that dark night

As I Lay Here

As I lay here and listen to the crickets
Watching the moonlight dance across the cornfield
I see the silhouette of the barn
I understand the peace that falls within here

Reconciliation gratefully has visited here
Only you Lord are here and I am here
Can we look at each other and understand
The influence Your hand has had

The fog lies on the stream
Brightly illuminated it shines as a beacon
Guiding hearts and minds
To a place of joy long lost

Prayers of gratitude shared by all
Hearts rejoice at the renewed
The treasure of time rediscovered
Freedom has spawned a place of peace

Circular Life

Circular life makes itself known
Worry free rays mingle with early morning mist
Sweet fragrance drifts across my path
My senses alive, new rain has freshened

Newly fledged bluebirds take turns
Dropping from branches valiantly snatching moths
Adult birds are ever vigilant nearby
Learn fast the air has a new scent

Yellow leaves create a collage on the green
Single acorns drop signaling the change
Their earthward decent marked by the leaves they smack
Dew covered spider webs adorn bushes

A great blue heron glides serenely overhead
HIS proud mocking bird charms the quiet
The repetitive call of the Cooper's hawk accentuates
All this day as the circle continues.

People Walk

Here in this park people walk, people hike
Surrounded by HIS handiwork
A man walks head down focused on the ground
2 small children buzz by on bike

Oblivious to the magnificent life around they gawk
A woman with 3 aged dogs passes, her best friends
Some walk as a social event chatting all the way
Most nod, few smile, several speak, but they walk

None notice tiny spider spinning its intricate creation
The deer alert and watching from the shadows
A lady stricken stops to talk
All different, all walking, many missing the show

Toddler grasping the sides of the stroller, eyes wide
Perhaps she sees more than most
Grand popular trees tower and offer shade
What a shame so many just walk!

The Lesson Plan

What a blessing we have in Her
A friend asked, was your Mom a teacher
Oh many were the ways some subtle some not so
Bed time prayer gave way to morning, beds made

Rise early, a full breakfast, all pitched in
Dad fed and watered the livestock
All 7, out the door in a rush such calamity
All with clean sharp dress and groomed just so

Days numbered by laundry, seam-stressing, house cleaning
Group activities of gardening, preserving, yard work
Musical instrument practice was not optional
Homemade animal shape birthday cakes and friends over

Lessons designed by HIM, spouse with ALS
Daily personal care, meals, health care demands
Sacrifice not known by most, deep love shown
What a blessing bestowed to all

HIS presence ever centered in all
Help one another, be kind, work hard, push boundaries
All taught while learning life's priorities
Yes teacher, yes Mom, yes a blessing!

The Leader

A mans man he is in all; Husband, Dad, Friend, grandpa, great pap pap
Quick with a smile and complement
So willing to do whatever for anyone, anytime
Always helping,doing, building, making for others

Truly lessons in motion if you watch
Move a family several states, OK when?
Plant 2000 seedlings, OK when?
Build a log cabin, OK when?

HIS Servant leadership in the purest form
Disagree with some but prays for them
Appreciates everything and quick with a thank you
Family time is his favorite, the more the merrier

Time takes it toll as with any but add ALS
Not a hill for a climber with HIM, ALS OK when?
The lessons taught are endless and the students many
A mans man he is in all; Husband, Dad, Friend, grandpa, great pap pap

The ER

So many beeps and tones
Drown out by the chatter from all directions
Gurneys come and go
Furrowed brows are common

A highway patrol accompanies one
Just then HIS quiet out of the blue
Time for a chest X-ray
Doc comes in, assessed, leaves

New arrivals at a steady pace
The questions the same the responses vary
No real personal space it's wide open
Folks working hard with great attitudes

Ahhh rest,hard to come by, but prevails
Pain is evidenced by the moans
The endless banter drones on
Second only to the beeps and tones.

Crisp Autumn Morning

The crisp autumn air floats down the mountain side
Sun's rays gently grace the colorful wall
A welcome process warming the earth
As a lone deer meanders only to quietly vanish in the wood

The roosters compete and their crassness shatters the silence
A grey squirrel eagerly gathers the plentiful acorns
Added to a well stocked stash in a tree
A distant dog proclaims it's presence

In a nearby pasture a horses nicker can be heard
The leaves begin to show their hidden fall brilliance
Some trees already scant with foliage
The pond is subdued by the chill and placid

The fall temperatures confronts comfort
Only to be reminded how alive we are in HIS garden
The sun now more abundant begins
As the crisp autumn air surrounds

Pre Dawn Sky

This pre dawn sky so bright
Stars ablaze, not a cloud
The moon so brilliant it chromes the yard
Quiet surrounds, blinking lights of a jogger pass

The crisp air greets my nose
Drone of traffic dominates the distant
Fall aromas filter through the air
Leaves, grass, humus all assault my senses

Can't help but wonder as the stars individual
How many are looking who, when, where,see, saw
Are we communal, indeed deep,
More similar than different, focus on

How humble does one feel looking up
As the moon moves the seasons do
Embrace and consume the change, become
HIS pre dawn sky so amazing

LIFE

How healthy is a nation that rationalizes death
HIS most precious sent on to Glory by evil
Prayer, Prayer, Prayer people wake up
Nations deteriorate, morals decline, rationalize? Really?

Those that pass by averting their eyes
Others defiantly holler pro choice with a fist
Yet some thumbs down, all believe they are right
Finally a coarse and emotional outburst

10 fold were the affirmations
Thumbs up, horn toots, a blessing hand held high
Some roll down the window, "God Bless you"
Thanks for what you are doing is heard

A choice, hardly, that was prior
A precious life, to be childlike the challenge
Difficult, such pervasive evil, devolves an entire nation
How does a nation survive that kills defenseless unborn?

The November Wood

Here in this November wood
Softly HIS cool gentle drops quench
The canopy is vastly irrelevant
Understory dominated by yellow
Lower yet green of various shades

A fly catcher darts into a deadfall
Squirrels eagerly forage in the leaf litter
The not so distant highway reminds me
Nature and her ways seem to be second

Remaining leaves reluctantly relinquish
Prodded by drops they search their rest
A chipmunk watches from a split tree
Dry and safe witnessing the beauty

Wet timber towers dark and strong
Their foliage created a mosaic carpeting
A pair of pileated woodpeckers crack the silence
All here in this November wood

Prayer

The power of prayer
Illusive for some unaware
Known by many who engage
Aid for those who need

Ask one terminal and suffering
Sure I / we pray daily for HIS mercy and peace
Comfort long sought seldom present
The bite of pain interrupts the hours

Requesting, offering, talking with HIM
Love the epicenter always
Neophytes amazed, become believers
It works, becomes their mantra

Empty offers of thoughts and prayers
Often abound, trite it may seem
Sincere and genuine ushers welcome change
The unfailing power of prayer

Tradition

A collection of memories
Recalled recited embellished laughed
Rich and storied shared effortlessly
One generation graciously give the next

Love the impetus
Annual trecks to that special place
Autumn ushers in the opportunity
With its dependable pervasive change

Leaves and all things green wither
Their transition to earth a reminder
HIS plan for all to return to love
The aroma of the transition guarantees spring

Smiles,hugs, laughter abound
Such cherished times so anticipated
Slow to happen,pass in a blink
Embrace those collections, share, love, live

The South 40

The melody of the stream drenches the air
The scent of Freshly harvested old pine rides the breeze
Cattle softly call to their young
Hardwoods ring the pasture like sentinels

The pastures lush thick green Long gone
The sun well on it's decent looses its splendor and warmth
The air shows it's characteristic December nip
The ground sponge like with recent rainfall

Coyote tracks along the stream betray their stealth
The breeze picks up the nip becomes a bite
A large rock sits defiantly in the middle of the pasture
Winter bluebirds drop in turn from the branches

HIS pine covered hill touches the blue sky
Crows repeat their seemingly endless harsh call
Several wild rose stems,beauty gone, wiggle in the breeze
All here in December on the south 40.

The Transition

The fight was long and heroic
He said he had to die to live
Live, smell the roses, everyday, all day
Genuine smiles dominated his expression, gratitude his position

"I pray for a peaceful death" he said, it was as wished
All left in this world sad but rejoicing for his new life with HIM
3 viewings packed,standing in the rain, accentuated by prayer and chant
Kind words, flowers, Mass cards, sympathy cards and donations overflowed

So proud he was looking down on his spouse and 7
Sitting in the front pew, together placing the pall
Individually, head held high participating, not sobbing
What a tribute, a packed church and a personal homily artfully delivered

Full military honors, all salute as the casket passed
A jolting 21 gun salute sounded off
Softly Taps drift through the air
Snappy, crisp and reverent flag folding marked the end of the valiant fight

HE Is

You know HE is as you see
It is all around you every day
Do you see the new life as eternal love
Leaves come and go with enthusiasm

Perry-winkle blossoms appear from the dirt
Daffodils pop up with vigor and brilliance
Defying the chill of the morn to greet you
Do you see HIM in the least living organism

Appreciate the bright cheer in the many bird songs
Red camellias shine forth as advocates for life
The scent of life dominates the air
Purple crocuses leap from the ground in splendor

The overwhelming abundance of life around you
Is far more evidence than any scripture that HE is
The first Bible awaits you every day
You know HE is as you see

The Morning Dance

It begins early, the morning dance
As the first rays pirouette breaking day
A fierce wind rushes on stage dominating the senses
Leaves skip across the pasture as if they are late

Crows scream their crass notes
Dipping and diving they seem to dance In the wind
Gracefully they conquer what seems unforgiving
Gusts deeply roar in the tree tops proclaiming their strength

Seemingly without notice what resembles a faint gobble
Pausing separating sound,parsing, yes another
The dance begins,trading notes we coax each other
HIS spring ritual in full display

The stream joins and taps out a melody on the rock
Hidden near cover a rainbow trout strikes
Dancing on its tail we celebrate together
Life in the present with creation is a marvelous morning dance

May I

The vertical shafts of various grey
Contrast sharply with the sea of green
Each reaching in unison to HIS light
Birds of every type carelessly flit and sing

Honeysuckle twists its way upward
Occasionally the Scent of wild roses delights
Evidence of the perpetual cycle abundant
The ground covered with once green leaves

As they become nourishment for the new green
A large black beetle forges in the rich forest floor
Randomly left then right like a pigeon in the plaza
For what I'll not know but wish him well

New plants of all shapes and sizes Jump as if to ask may I
Playing a critical role in HIS cosmic plan
A grey squirrel hops, jumps and darts frantically searching
All appreciate the verticals shafts of various grey and green work of art.

Spring Showers

The rhythm of steady rain greets the pre dawn
Yielding to an intense deluge then back again
Walking across a harvested cornfield a pair of ducks take flight
The day is breaking and HIS life inescapable

Hiking up a hill 2 deer are startled
Gracefully bounding to safety
The dense fragrance of the many autumn olive overwhelm the senses
The sweetness so thick it drips from every molecule like honey from a spoon

Songbirds inundate the silence with their endless notes
Three buck slowly feed across the field
Their antlers just beginning to grow In velvet
A gobbler announces his dominion with a thunderous call

The serenity of this place seeps into my soul
The collage of various colors, shapes and textures
Dogwood reluctantly free their petals
An indigo bunting, its brilliant azul proclaims the sacredness of here

Printed in the United States
By Bookmasters